# The Book of Emblems

# The Book of Emblems

Matthew Ladd

WAYWISER

First published in 2010 by

# THE WAYWISER PRESS

Bench House, 82 London Road, Chipping Norton, Oxon OX7 5FN, UK
P.O. Box 6205, Baltimore, MD 21206, USA
http://waywiser-press.com

Editor-in-Chief
Philip Hoy

Senior American Editor
Joseph Harrison

Associate Editors
Clive Watkins   Greg Williamson

Copyright © Matthew Ladd, 2010

The right of Matthew Ladd to be identified as the author of this work
has been asserted by him in accordance with the
Copyright, Designs and Patents Act of 1988.

All rights reserved

A CIP catalogue record for this book is available from the British Library

ISBN 978-1-904130-43-7

Printed and bound by
TJ International Ltd, Padstow, Cornwall

*To my family*

# Acknowledgments

Grateful acknowledgment is made to the following publications in which these poems first appeared, sometimes in earlier versions:

*Antioch Review*: "Coelacanth"
*Bellevue Literary Review*: "Ancestors," "The Rise and Fall of Christianity in Santa Fe"
*Cellpoems*: "Little Ghazal"
*Gulf Coast*: "Fountain of the Planet of the Apes"
*New Letters*: "Descent"
*Paris Review*: "The Traveling Dissection Tent"
*Southern Review*: "The Funeral Supper," "Scenes From a Party"
*Virginia Quarterly Review*: "Appalachian Diurnal"
*Yale Review*: "Dreaming in German," "Poem for K."

# Contents

*Foreword by Rosanna Warren*     11

Envoi     17

## I

| | |
|---|---|
| Margaret at Home | 21 |
| Scene from the *Iliad* | 22 |
| Discourse on Phenomenology | 23 |
| Imitation | 24 |
| Poem for K. | 25 |
| La Vie Militaire | 26 |
| Yes, Virginia | 29 |
| Scenes From a Common Life | 30 |

## II

| | |
|---|---|
| The Funeral Supper | 39 |
| The Rise and Fall of Christianity in Santa Fe | 40 |
| Fighting the Devil Without, Fighting the Devil Within | 41 |
| Marcel Proust's Last Summer Holiday | 44 |
| Hölderlin Alone | 45 |
| Scenes from a Party | 46 |
| Ancestors | 48 |
| Little Ghazal | 49 |
| The Animal Kingdom | 50 |
| The French Surrealist at the Operating Theatre | 51 |

## III

| | |
|---|---|
| Growing Older as a Kind of Civics Lesson | 57 |
| The Traveling Dissection Tent | 58 |

*Contents*

| | |
|---|---|
| And the Merciful Harrow Grew Dull | 59 |
| Fountain of the Planet of the Apes | 60 |
| Is It the Quiet Mind that Calls | 61 |
| Dreaming in German | 62 |
| Appalachian Diurnal | 64 |
| Klintholm Havn | 66 |

IV

| | |
|---|---|
| Elegy for J.S. Mill | 69 |
| Descent | 74 |
| Coelacanth | 75 |

| | |
|---|---|
| *A Note About Matthew Ladd* | 77 |
| *A Note About the Anthony Hecht Poetry Prize* | 79 |

# Foreword by Rosanna Warren

"The history books have ripened into fables," the prematurely aged poet announces in the "Envoi" opening *The Book of Emblems*. A fin de siècle, elegant, ironic weariness colors these poems. "The coat is not modern; I am not modern; / you see I am concerned with modernity," declares the speaker in the sequence "Scenes From a Common Life." The life described is anything but common, and it unfurls under the tutelary gaze of James Merrill, whose patrician manners and tone have helped to shape Ladd's poems.

But Matthew Ladd uses the wit he has learned from Merrill to hold Merrill at bay ("... No argument here, / though he's a far cry, say, from Merrill's *Changing Light*", "Scenes From a Common Life"), as he uses deftness borrowed from Larkin to summon and dismiss that master: "but because Larkin is such an unrepentant asshole / and for all that, still beautiful // like an aging circus performer ..." ("Imitation") – where the rhyme of "asshole" and "beautiful" clinches the argument. In ringing the changes on his elders, Ladd begins to strike notes recognizable as no one's but his own.

This is a young man's book. It flaunts its youth, partly, in the pose of ironic detachment, as though a cycle of sentimental education had been completed. As indeed it has, no doubt. The poet who tell us, "I am lying here, practicing self-love" (in "Scene from the *Iliad*") has emancipated himself from at least one set of romantic illusions. Two aesthetics vie for dominance. One, the mode of Parnassian charm, is almost too successful, and if relied on too much could doom its author to a minor, decorative Mannerism. This is the voice that opens "Poem for K.": "'... a time of thick Bearnaise and mercenary quibbling,' / the tutor concluded..." But Ladd is made of stronger stuff. A tougher vision gathers force through these pages. It is voiced, often, in curt declarations, synaptic leaps, and precise, economical observations; its labor is to locate a center of consciousness through a survey of reductions. Ladd's honed metrics serve him well; in "Scenes From a Common Life," one of the key achievements of the collection, the blank verse goes about its business with an insouciant, purposeful mastery:

*Foreword by Rosanna Warren*

I am twenty-seven years old; the god is not in me;
    all my possessions the dried-up fructure of books,
translucent wool sweaters, matchbooks stowed in mint-tins
    and a photograph of my father at my age, the steam of his tea
twining around the smoke of a cigarette.
    My life pulled from the ashes: realm of the present.

The quality of Ladd's seeing, as much as his voicing, guarantees his staying power. He glances into the nature of things. There are his potato beetles "… with liver-spotted shells / picking along the doorscreen on soft hooked feet" ("The Animal Kingdom"). There is "the salted grain of the boardwalk" ("Scenes From a Common Life"). There are storms "with their million-fingered waves" ("Appalachian Diurnal"), and, in "Klintholm Havn," the lovely waves that "bare their backs / and melt into foam." All of these observations, sensuous and just in themselves, are strategically placed, and pulsate with symbolic suggestion.

With *The Book of Emblems*, a new poet steps out into the public square, by turns dashing, modest, canny, stylish, whimsical, and stern. And though one of his avatars may lie in bed practicing self-love, this maestro, through his many guises, reveals himself as admirably free from self-infatuation. That romance having been set aside, there is no telling where Ladd's many gifts will lead him. The horizon is wide.

– Rosanna Warren

Swann had now only to enter the concert-room, the doors of which were thrown open to him by an usher loaded with chains, who bowed low before him as though tendering to him the keys of a conquered city. But he thought of the house in which at that very moment he might have been, if Odette had but permitted, and the remembered glimpse of an empty milk-can upon a door-mat wrung his heart.

– Marcel Proust, *Swann's Way*

> Above the marvel, each rigid head,
> Angels, their unnatural wings displayed,
> Freeze into an attitude
> Recalling the dead.

– Geoffrey Hill, "Picture of a Nativity"

## Envoi

Our open windows usher in the cold.
    The market falls, and gentle tycoons
postpone their vacations. A billion children flock
    to well-protected dunes

where one can watch the ridleys lay their eggs,
    then leave before they swim away.
Each night is a boat, unmoored, that spins and drifts
    into a waiting day

that disillusions no one. No stray wind
    erases the eye of your cigarette,
and Saturdays once mad with Chardonnay
    are pacified and quiet.

The history books have ripened into fables.
    Only a few old men, their hair-
less heads drawn down in collars of soft wool,
    play hearts in a leaf-strewn square.

I

## Margaret at Home

Intelligence in a beautiful house is power.
When you watch the building of a beautiful house,
you see intelligence running through its timbers.
Its slate gables preside from heights
Buddhistic in their benevolence,
and its doors, like judicious sentinels,
reject the unenlightened guest.
The finished house is a prefix,
rattling off empty facts in a sleep
that diverts grief as easily as rain.

But you! You wake like a needle
pulled from a block of white wax,
from the dream of a solidly built foundation.
Then the curtains are parted
on the ringing fortress of night
and you see what has always been before you:
three dahlias in a vase of water
and, farther out, the hills of northern Kentucky.

## Scene from the *Iliad*

Alone on an April morning.
A neighbor coughs into his hand.
Indistinguishable fragments of conversation
drift from passing schoolchildren.

I am lying here, practicing self-love.
In the *Iliad*, a man with a leather buckler
drives the length of a ten-foot spear
through another man's eye socket.

A slip of red smoke lets itself out.
The breastplate sighs, the sandals loosen.
Who will remember my death
but the one who causes it?

# Discourse on Phenomenology

Hell is for those who see it.
For some, the burning wasp-track
is merely an eddy of red leaves,
the choking tunnel of dung a hedgerow
where sparrows and nightjars cluster.

This, at least, is what we are told.
It is only a question of perspective:
change your life, the world changes with it.
The atavisms embraced by our elders
will not be reborn in our children.

I lift the door-latch. *Satan! A linden tree!*

# Imitation

When I read Philip Larkin
and picture him mugging to Kingsley about WATCHING SCHOOL-
                                                       GIRLS
or Jamaican WOGS hawking used clothes in Brixton,
I know this is the year zero

all over again, not because
people haven't changed, or English poets,
but because Larkin is such an unrepentant asshole
and for all that, still beautiful,

like an aging circus performer.
Why are the old so difficult to forgive?
What kind of place have we come to, really,
where doubt racks us like a bad cough

and human feet wash up with the sea-swill,
a few more or less than the day before?
Someone must write it all down, I suppose,
even if no one reads the moldering notebook

whose dowdy author so swiftly convicted himself ...
"And immediately rather than words ..." Ah, Philip,
how impossible the accurate naming of things:
cathedrals, children, the blank self-regard of the bachelor.

# Poem for K.

"... a time of thick Bearnaise and mercenary quibbling,"
the tutor concluded, clicking the slide to whiteness.
He always had some salient *mot* for Father,
and he had read enough of Sir James Frazer
to crack a few jokes about pricked foreskin.
"Take my *Homo catullus*, please!" he would say,
or "Heavens! All that vulgar chamois upholstery!"
Like overzealous critics, we lampooned his serge blazers
and ambled about the Arno's marble bollards,
darker than darkness, clever and querulous,
one eye on the weather and the other on each other.
In Copenhagen, at Andersen's cenotaph,
we ate cheese sandwiches and pickled eggs.
In London, the Queen's Guards with their milk-can shakos
stiffened their sabers between our stage-gargoyle faces.

Why did you leave? Was it our view of the Thames
disgorging dead fish like a greenhorn river-god?
That winter, the Brent iced over, its oilskin surface
brittle as mica, tragic, ephemeral.
You settled in Boston, studied, grew sharp as a needle.
How frustrating to realize the distance between us ...
first that failed picnic on the Shuttlecock Terrace,
and now this lukewarm tea, not to mention
my gaffe at last week's chamber concert –
I don't think your husband will ever forgive me.
Your hand, that once rocked my cradle,
rocks so contentedly, these late days, another.
But I wanted only for us to talk like friends again,
K., K., my long-lost, best-loved sister.

# La Vie Militaire

### I. Song

Clinking of empty bottles between the sheets.
Female odors fleeing the bed, damp pillows.
He wakes with his rifle's muzzle
nestled under his chin.
From the crenellated minarets,
the morning call to prayer.

*A house made of bones*
*is shelter.*

There was a run on the bank.
This bank, however,
was not a Money Bank
but a Politeness Bank.
Everyone withdrew the exact amount
he or she was owed by the others.

*A city made of wood*
*is shelter.*

"I am still looking for a German
with whom I might be able to be serious
in my own way ..." Over coffee,
the soldiers discuss this part of the essay.
They never remember the second part –
the part about being cheerful!

*A house made of bones*
*is shelter.*
*A city made of wood*
*is shelter.*
*A human body*
*is shelter.*

*La Vie Militaire*

## II. Poem

Start small: a pip.
Now a plate of pips:
mandarin, lemon, soursop.
Now a cluster
of Queen Anne's lace,
a blip
on the radar of an RAF pilot.

Now the pilot getting pipped
in the windpipe by a plug of shrap-
nel, roughly the size and shape
of a scarab beetle.
Pip-pop-pip.
His fingers fly to his neck.
The biplane tailspins,
dives into the jungle.

## III. Story

Here in the desert, there is no pratique
to govern who comes and goes.
One avoids certain streets at certain hours.
The dead seem no more quiet than the living:
the boy in the white burnous,
the girl in the black silk yashmak.

The seismograph trembles in its glass casing.
Some new creature is making its approach.
Can it be that what we fear most
is not ineffable, but entirely self-evident
and thus not worth bothering about?
When Christ died, the Romans cast lots for his clothing.

*La Vie Militaire*

Here in the desert, there are no monkeys,
unlike that film in which mad Klaus Kinski,
alone on a raft of rotting Spaniards,
roars at imaginary interlocutors
as the capuchins hop nimbly into the river.
Like him, we descend into nothing

through dense foliage.

# Yes, Virginia

Yes, Virginia, they *do* shoot horses.
They do it with pearl-handled pistols
there on the racetrack, or out of sight in the pastures,

and when newspaper editors start to exhibit
signs of weakness, they'll shoot a few of those,
though hardly ever in the United States.

Does that clear things up for you? It's no use
going into the gory details, really;
I know how upsettable you girls can be!

But here's something I hope you'll remember
while the long summer burns and your charmed life
unfurls like a pennant of blessings before you:

that sleep is a gift, and mercy necessary,
and love between man and woman impossible.

# Scenes From a Common Life

### I. The Prodigal Son

March wind snakes through the pulley frames
    of my antediluvian bedroom windows.
Fear of losing one's roots? Separation anxiety.
    Fear of finding them again – too rare a problem
to merit a popular nomenclature. I settle back in bed.
    A tight-fisted ranch-house slides into my vision,
dragging along the topography
    that spawned all those names: Plainview, Littlefield,
Levelland. Fiefdoms of cotton and oil, "the richest land
    and the finest people." Eighteen hundred miles
northeast of it all, I wrap the blanket more tightly around me.
    My eyes cloud over; my lips harden like clay.

I am twenty-seven years old; the god is not in me;
    all my possessions the dried-up fructure of books,
translucent wool sweaters, matchbooks stowed in mint-tins
    and a photograph of my father at my age, the steam of his tea
twining around the smoke of a cigarette.
    My life pulled from the ashes: realm of the present.

### II. Sunday Morning

Sodalities of the Elk Lodge, whose members include
    two alcoholic uncles and an ex-best-friend,
whose mystic rites I visualized, as a child,
    as burning of camphor, as pastry-brushing
of thick elk-steaks, its lot now no more
    than an obstacle to be overstepped
on my way to a memorial, a Requiem Mass
    at St. Ignatius' Parish. Locusts chirr and leap
before me to the door. I sing and pray.
    And lacking the *joie de vivre* of the arthropod caste

lope home darkly. Read. *'What do you make of that?'* asked Holmes.
   *'The name of the maker, no doubt; or his monogram, rather.'*
I pluck a blue nosegay from my buttonhole.
   Christmas candles with fat waxed wicks
squat on the coffee table in gothic remonstrance.

*'To tell the truth'* – *he sank his face into his thin, white hands* –
*'I have felt helpless ... I seem to be in the grasp of some resistless,*
   *inexorable evil ...'* Isn't it always the innocent
who die too soon, shredded to confetti in the crossfire,
   capped in the throat by a comrade-in-arms with a price?
On the brink of manhood, I have wasted my days in poetry,
   my nights in the cultivation of questionable attachments.

Let the evening go, let it go. There will be others
   in which you are presented with a cassis and soda
in a cut-glass tumbler precisely to your liking
   and asked to develop your views on carbon emissions.
How exhausting to talk to people, regardless of the context!
   The minor flaws exposed, palms perspiring, deflection the
                                            rule of the day ...
What instruments are within my reach
   I take, and use them. That is the best defense I can offer.


III. High Comedy

Coney Island boardwalk. A steel gate guards the street. Ladd
                                            approaches
   gingerly. Bolted to the threshold, a missal stand
on which an antique book, smelling of linseed, lies open. He pauses,
   hesitates – *what language* – touches a page ...
*SNAP!* Bright teeth bury themselves in his wrist; up jumps a blood-
                                            bracelet.
   And through the salt-startled curtain of his eyes, the words

swim upward to satisfy, even now, his curiosity ... *Italian!* Another
    unreadable language! If only that year in Milan
he had proved more diligent ... A man
    in black hood and goatskin sandals
approaches, pauses, walks onward. Hours pass. Bleating Ladd
    recites a poem from his youth.
Cold comfort. The steel teeth stir, burrow more deeply.

    The shadows lengthen. He has drawn a small crowd.
No more cowled death's-heads, but a clump of onlookers
    as might step out 'for air' on Brighton Beach, c. 1910,
waifish kids in sailor's suits, corseted women with pouter-pigeons,
    beanpoles in knickers and flannel jackets – *God.* He feels
                                           like Christ
trapped in a Graham Greene story: half-drunk, unshaven,
    the pinnacle of health despite his best intentions.
(We must forgive him if, in the future, he sinks,
    leans back to light an apple clove, or rubs the scarred wrist
absently, as one might touch an old lover's
    comb-shell hairclip, hardly recalling its former purpose ...)

Twilight. The spring slackens, the teeth retreat.
    No one to see. He follows the salted grain of the boardwalk
                                      home.


## IV. Low Comedy

Situational comedy, they call it, when the best friend bursts in
    on his couch-bound housemates, stammers, "Ph-Phoebe
told me you guys were at Zabar's!" The dough-chested putz
    always making his move a second too early, too late
for the bespectacled girl at the coffee bar to notice ...
    Situational comedy: their jaunt through midtown Manhattan
a foretaste of paradise, where no one pays taxes or loses an arm

in a glass factory, or grows a few minutes older in a bathroom
reeking with iodine. He touches the black cotton to his wrist,
   like an apprentice to the Franciscan friars
in the ateliers of Assisi, mid-Trecento, famed for their mastery
   of colored glass! Yes, if he might capture
those luminous saints in the light of tripartite windows
   cut and leadlined, painted with the appropriate pigments,
vermilion for the Pietá's bright orgy of wounds,
   ultramarine for the Virgin, her straw-gold hair sticklighted
to achieve just the right texture and translucence, yes, *that*
   would be work to aspire to! Though there's no telling, for certain,
that this is how the great windows were made. Supreme irony:
   the monks never wrote it down. Situational comedy:
– *Where's Fra Filippo?*
   – *Dead, this morning.*
– *O Dio mio! He was to teach me the staining of glass!*


V. Intermezzo (Parable of Job)

Job napped behind a haywain, weak from debate.
   In the blink of his old god's eye, his fields
shed their quilts of heather, and turned from purple
   to burnt butterscotch. Every dead stalk
bent low to the ground with its own private burden;
   centuries passed; the lentil plots clicked through their seasons
like cuttlefish. Lucifer sharpened his knife on a stone.
   June broke in a scattershot of warblers. Job awoke.
And having lost everything in a past life, he drank from a stream
   and took up at last the mantle of the shramana.
In the pebbles pressed under his feet, in the bells of Brahmans,
   in the black power lines clattering like yellow-jackets,
he felt the unknowable, the unwriteable, what is left unrecorded
   for lesser minds to contemplate.

VI. The Romantic Sublime

These apricot-pink putti poised with cock-quill pens
    might as well be made of marzipan,
they are so cloying. Only children can stomach them.
    I much prefer the eleven-fingered clothier
jerked from obscurity by the needlework of his poems
    whose threads were woven so cleverly from his blindness …
Ah! For a life that stretches beyond the pale of vision –
    calendars built on arpeggios! Palm-readings!
The tropism of weekend rambles down the conservatory! There,
    in Jean-Jacques' *petit chateau*, are my beloved familiars
beginning with the thumb of pepper aquavit
    put out this morning on the cracked deal-table –
just enough to rob my tongue of its moisture.
    The gardeners in their denim blouses
treat me graciously, chanting, "We know what it's like
    to have the world at your feet, the pang of responsibility
that comes with years of hard work. Your enemies were wrong."
    In my herb garden, the lavender and fennel
soften the pathways and lighten the French sorrel.


VII. The Critic

    Once more, with feeling. Fate's limestone hand
briefly tightens on yours, then crumbles. Years ago,
    you thought it would crush the talent from you like oil,
your hand cold-pressed to death, proof-pressed to immortality.
    It is not so, not in your lifetime. The prestidigitations
of form you abandoned to 'language-play,' then retreated
    to the metrics of youth, those lyrical afternoons
squandered pumping out sonnets in the green room.
    Now, "L. sweetens his cynicism
with a charming, if puzzled, naiveté." No argument here,

    though he's a far cry, say, from Merrill's *Changing Light*,
whose powwows at the Ouija with Ephraim
    knit so seamlessly ratiocination, clairvoyance, faith in art
and our childlike desire for unfettered communion,
    the fumbling transparent, silly, and thereby lovely.

I stir up my coffee grounds with a pen, and get only
    the thirty-seventh and thirty-eighth views of Mount Fuji.

And I do not love all men and women equally,
    and I do not love all people equally.
Neither can I relax this week, as dust flecks the desktop
    like quicklime, and my father's cigarettes
beseech me from my shallow coat-pocket.
    The coat is not modern; I am not modern;
you see I am concerned with modernity.
    And also with truth, like everyone. The honeycomb
that thrives in the rotten belly of the lion,
    and the beetle's leg tap-tapping along my vitrine
like a crude wooden crutch kiss-kissing the stones of a street
    that winds through a seaside village in a bad Victorian novel.

II

## The Funeral Supper

To wit: crostini, red pears soaked in beef broth,
damp phyllo under cheesecloth, china bowls
of hand-pressed pastas – tortellini, gnocchi,
radiatori – almonds, balsamic, warm chèvre
for apricot canapés, white truffle glaze
to lighten the centerpiece (rosettes of lamb
with grilled asparagus-tips), twenty-five bottles
of good Bordeaux, and twenty of Pinot Blanc.

Once they'd released the servants and drawn chairs
in for the women, they ate and drank for hours
in silence. (The dogs and children slept.) By dawn,
the ravenous ghost of their dead friend had gone –
the soup-bones, bread-heels, salt rubbed into wine-stains
love's proof against guilt, the meal that keeps on eating.

# The Rise and Fall of Christianity in Santa Fe

There they worked hard, carving the doors and chairs
from walnut, cedar. Knobs of hammered tin
lay in a box; the masons smoked outside.
The carpenters spoke like disciples, in fearful whispers.
When their son followed his instinct into the river,
they could believe in God, believe the current
that swallowed him was real, a fickle wind
that coughed him up two hundred yards downstream.

She turns and disappears. He drives three nails
into a loosening post, between whose rails
he sees the river dry, their sheep returning.
Her face is gone, remains gone, is replaced
by lamps, the finished home. It watches out
for what would cross the plain, at night, to wake him.

## Fighting the Devil Without, Fighting the Devil Within

Another year has ended with the rumble of guns.
Another has begun the same way. The honey locust
drops its soft pods like a tired tar baby;
the winter wheat mutters and chuffs from the roadside.
My answer, fragile as wet lambskin,
still manages to warm two frozen boulders
that fling themselves lustily over the precipice
like demon swine. Is theirs the pious speech
of D. Alighieri, his back to a Ghibelline forest,
its floor as damp and treacherous as San Marco's?
No use in asking. I've studied enough logic
to distinguish synthetic from analytic truths –
these trees are neither. They are lachrymose trees.
The Chinese use them to glaze teacups.

I am an economist, tracking the global black market.
Rhino-horn dagger-hafts buffed with jism
command outrageous prices in the Persian Gulf;
the D.R.C. sees juntas, mass executions ...
But you already know all this.
Your heart is pure as crystal.
I'd thought that no one would try to corrupt you
as long as your forehead bore that cross of ash,
but you were so conspicuous, hurrying to the piazza
at dawn for your seat at the evening executions –
poor ingénue! They hadn't even brought the scaffolding.
Let us walk instead to the botanic gardens.
The nasturtiums will be blooming this time of year,
and the hothouses may be open.

*Yes, yes, such ceilings of soft, green glass!*
*How many forgotten sanctuaries there must be in the world,*
*where the sun falls diagonally into the vestibules*
*and artisans' names are chiseled into the plinths!*
*How I would love to tour such palaces as these,*

*Fighting the Devil Without, Fighting the Devil Within*

*or pay the nominal fee to sleep for one night*
*in their magnificent carved oak four-posters!*
*You see, I am not exactly the lost boy*
*my competitors imagine. I am a humble lecturer*
*brought up in distant view of the Pyrenees.*
*By this you may believe in the optimism*
*for which I have become quite famous.*
*Next week I am attending a conference*
*in East Berlin; everyone knows me there ...*

You must stay alert and keep always on your guard.
For someone is always sidling up to you in a silk cloak
or similar costume, whispering, "Of course, my friend,
they don't understand Schopenhauer like *we* do."
That is the man you must watch out for.
In Mombasa, for instance, I took coffee with ground ginger
from a bored and bearded street-vendor
who asked for nothing but my money.
I knew there was no poison in the cup.
And you may be anemic, and rise dizzily
from the walnut parquetry of your landing,
but you've also memorized a little Auden
(the crowds like harvest wheat, the tiny glacier)
and can recite it to yourself in troubled times.

Here, January drones on like a forgotten fermata.
The hog-faced rabbits kick in their sleep.
Nothing for miles but houses of toothpicks and spit,
their belvederes fluttering with scraps of baize,
their walls mosaicked with Dover Thrift dustcovers.
*Are you trying to learn that music?*
*It's quite difficult, I assure you.*
Where the Apollo Theater once stood,
a fire-pit, a windbreak of poplars. It is a setting
I shall remember when writing my prospectus

*Fighting the Devil Without, Fighting the Devil Within*

for the imaginary opera I am now in charge of.
Dear Father: What a surplus of apothegms
you gave me on my twenty-seventh birthday.
They've slipped through my fingers, every one.

# Marcel Proust's Last Summer Holiday

Balbec's only historical marker
is a 16<sup>th</sup>-century iron starboard anchor
half-buried in a hectare of Pinot Grigio.

No one goes there. The fishmongers congregate
in martini bars inland from the old city
to drink pastis and sleep with each others' daughters.

In April, a toxic luminescent algae
masses like crown fire atop the breakers;
fish wash up and are shoveled into wheelbarrows.

And when you visit, three months out of the year,
you rarely need to ask questions. Everything
is answered for you already, the gate unlatched,

the shutters pushed open. You confess
things are not always as you remember:
the stalls still prop their skate-wings in beds of ice,

but L'Auberge des Oiseaux, over the off-season,
has renamed itself *Le Harlequin Hotel*.
Marcel, forgive them. You, too, will end up a liar.

# Hölderlin Alone

His nails grew long, as if to track his madness.
It frightened the sane: the Tübingen carpenter
who took him in, the pale and savage students
whose taunts he met by hurling shit and rocks,
the woman he loved, whose soft refusals fell
like blessings from her window. When the poems
clotted his tongue, he would walk out to free them,
would don his tweeds and pace the Neckar River.
Young mothers with their children paused to watch him,
the way he used small bits of wood or leather
as interlocutors for his tête-à-têtes
with spirits, old professors, brothel girls.

The year *Phänomenologie des Geistes*
was printed, he ventured deeper than his friend
and broke the surface rarely – just to play
snatches of Schiller, or write long, lucid letters
to his dead mother. Through his attic walls
came eloquent sirens of the Gott-an-Ich.
They thrilled him to the hundredth inward turn –
in his own face he saw their tongueless speech,
and heard the Neckar draining to the Rhine
in waves of blood that washed against his bone.

## Scenes from a Party

... and late the evening goes,
until they've stained the tablecloth's thin skin
into a Rorschach blot of wine on linen.
David declares it a "massive Shroud of Turin";
Jean dashes off a bourrée,
then tackles the Tchaikovsky *Barcarolle*.
Marcus distributes figs from a golden bowl.

The moon passes overhead.
Through dusty rooms, an ancient chocolate Lab –
eyes gone, ears useless – stalks elusive scents
that lure him like a lover's blandishments.
Back in the dining room,
Dennis and Jack play hockey with baguettes
and pucks of filet mignon. Upstairs, Anne lets

Kevin unbutton her shirt.
Jean, fighting stupor, plugs away at a rondo.
The moon wanes. Milk glass, in a hutch whose doors
are lattices of finest crystal, pours
pink light on the oak divan
on which lies sleeping, conquered by the drab,
gray, sadly scentless attic, the chocolate Lab.

Oblivion is now
by its deaf reckoning: as the morning sun
peeks dazzlingly in seconds from the hill
to wash the stains of sleep from boy and girl
and drowsing dog, a night
already stirs bone-deep in each. What these
cobbled-together kingdoms of their bodies

*Scenes from a Party*

will do to keep the peace!
The house, reposing, is like some frail beast
lying reflective in a pool of shade:
Kevin and Anne, in a bed rudely unmade,
Marcus, mouth dribbling figs,
Alice in watered silk, stretched out on the lawn,
a few dead robins on the terrace. Dawn

breaks. The party over,
each guest wakes to furnishings more real
than those remembered – finds the rooms repaired
to wreck, the linens stained, the table smeared
with what, last night, was pure
unfettered genius – to brave the morning's blind
white covenant, more puzzling than unkind.

## Ancestors

Packed away now, face-down in styrofoam,
my grandmother's antebellum tintypes hung
for years in her entrance-hall, reflecting the guests
who passed before them like novitiates.
Her grandfather – a young surgeon in the war –
had lifted them off men with whom he'd fought
at Malvern Hill and Manassas under Lee,
and then Antietam, where "But for the grace
of Christ our Lord," she said, "he had died like them."

When I was old enough, my father would take me
to visit her in the home. He rarely spoke,
content (I thought) to watch her withered hands
stroking the home's teak rocker, swirling ice
to lukewarm whirlpools in her glass of tea.
I worshipped and feared her in a child's way –
entranced by the sour, rich odors of her skin.
She seemed to wear some opiate perfume
distilled from her family's beautiful dead women.

I thought, too, that the tintypes must be those
of *my* ancestors, uncles whose blue blood
I might taste once I'd joined the hallowed list
of names I pictured filling the scrolls of heaven –
Malachi Croft, Elijah Birchfield.

My father has put them under styrofoam.
But they, like patients under chloroform,
exhale a fog that lingers low and cold
and smells of trampled corn, in that Maryland field
that rose to receive them from the stunning volleys.

# Little Ghazal

Summer sirocco razing
fallow land to beaten copper.

Herd of Brangus, horns
like speckled whalebone,

fat-swollen dewlaps
heavy as fruitbread.

Your only birthmark –
a Hindu mandala, left hip.

Fosters all sorts
of grade-school serendipities:

*Two-floor flat with fanlight,*
*Chippenham Mews, ring mornings.*

Rosemary's scrub through March;
by April, muggy and lusty.

So flourish your emery-
coated tongue depressor

in praise of Folly, bad muse,
worse Junior Inquisitor.

Legion of dust devils
in luckless Job's harmattan;

Sawed-off shottie
primed for the black reynard.

# The Animal Kingdom

I despise the swallows that nest in my chimney.
For company, I prefer potato beetles:
comic bunglers with liver-spotted shells

picking along the doorscreen on soft hooked feet.
I honor their approach to health and mortality.
When the swallows crush them, they die happy.

My name hangs from a hook in my father's study.
I ride my bicycle through a rain-slick city
where nothing is ugly, awful, or jaw-shattering.

My friends, this world, I see it is changing.
Our parents age like foods under heat-lamps;
a clicking announces itself, sickness.

The soft cameras that nourished us are yawning
and putting on their velvet caps.
We seek order, find only dereliction.

Out of the bedsheet, a brown spider finds
it loves the feel of a cold human hand.
It needs no language for loving this way,

no staying power. Only an eye
for marking what others would ignore:
a crevice, a cry, a hemisphere.

# The French Surrealist at the Operating Theatre

Watching Glenn Gould play the piano
is like being present at the vivisection
of some enormous, white-fleshed creature.
The audience cranes forward
in its cracked leather seats,
trained on the performer's hands
lifting their ten long scalpels
in the glare of the klieg lights ...

There we are witness to a concert
in which no music is heard and no one speaks;
it seems as if the stage itself is waiting
for death, for the entrance of a chorus.
The drumbeat echoes itself
more faintly with each drawn breath.
We have come to understand life
by what it cannot give us.

\* \* \*

New myths clamber daily into the life-raft;
each day buzzes with the rumors of coups.
I do not want them, I am far too old.
Leave me my photographs of Turkish women
lounging open-legged on damask couches.

\* \* \*

Night falls on a prehistoric forest.
Behind the painted stage-curtain, the jaguar growls:
*Where do we come from? What are we?*

\* \* \*

*The French Surrealist at the Operating Theatre*


A swimming pool on the city's northeast suburb
is rumored to possess healing properties.
A woman leads her son, a blind infant,
to its concrete lip and drops him in by the ankles.
Miraculous – he already knows how to swim!

I must be honest with you: not once
have I doubted the existence of God
in the minds of his followers.

\* \* \*


The ghost of Glenn Gould gathered itself on the horizon.
*Who else,* I demanded, *have you led on
through this droll waste of ivory and plaster?
Only you, my friend,* he replied,
*you and ten thousand others.*

\* \* \*


When adjectives misplace themselves
then turn up grinning in a drawer or an herb garden,
is it acceptable to laugh, and hack them to pieces?

\* \* \*


Guillaume Apollinaire! I know where you sleep,
I have drifted along the Faubourg St. Germain
to the music of coughing syphilitics –
I have reckoned myself against the abyss
that swirls like the sea in the Russian filmmaker's pupil –
I have curled in the lees of slump-blocks

*The French Surrealist at the Operating Theatre*

not once doubting the purpose of my exertions –
I have come home to a quiet apartment
and filled the teakettle, and typed out my letters –
I have lived alone these many lonely years.

Why then do you not answer me?
I shall be bold, Guillaume, and demand an explanation,
you garlanded satyr, gatekeeper of the lascivious ...
I am not like you, I am not one of you.
If I called myself a revolutionary,
it would only be for want of companionship.

\* \* \*

What right have we not to be acting on instinct?
The present century has not eviscerated us,
nor do its satellites offer any information
that is not lovely from certain odd angles.
Witness the Yongbyon cooling tower
bleeding steam for decades before its destruction.

\* \* \*

I had to postpone my Grand Tour
to care for my ailing mother.

When, after long years, she passed on,
I was too old to travel.

I sat for hours in her black kitchen chair
dreaming my life's lost adventure.

III

# Growing Older as a Kind of Civics Lesson

In the Year of Absolute Reassessment,
the President announced
the end of all presidencies.
White-gloved cadets
fell on their bayonets
and zealous Ivy Leaguers
wrote to perplexed mothers,
"Mother, do not look for me,
for I am already home."
The factories closed early
to celebrate new holidays.
Our mayor snipped the ribbons
on colorful government buildings,
and there prevailed about our city
a general despondency.

In that year, a wandering eye
could get you a month in prison.
Why, then, did we gather
in the vacant homes of strangers
to explore each other sexually?
You see I am writing here
of you, Emily, you and me.
There were no others
in that hall of mirrors,
in that year of living secretively,
when the speaker-boxes in the public squares
called me from my soliloquies,
no longer to speak, but to listen.

## The Traveling Dissection Tent

The traveling dissection tent is gone.
The stakes are pulled, the mason jars are cracked
and crusted with formaldehyde. The lawn
is a brown slab. I lie down. I am packed
with gauze and dusty air that lets me sail
inside myself – until I am alive,
my feet in scalpel-oil, the spicy trail
of fluid on the sheet ... We would arrive
at dusk, and stay, and watch.
                                        I want her back.
I want the Lady in the Smock. She smelled
like buttermilk and almonds. Father told
me not to tell, but late one night he took
her hand. They walked outside the tent, and I –
I touched the body's skin, and closed its eye.

# And the Merciful Harrow Grew Dull

As a child, I dreaded water. I could not swim, would not bathe
                              alone, and enjoyed only
   listening to my mother's lullabies, which I sang to myself after
                                        her death.

Singing in that voice reminded me of her hands: how, when she
                                        grew angry,
   they swooped like gulls over an empty beach, unable to rest.

Her phonograph ran down. We had no extra needles. Each morning,
                                    my father dressed
   and assembled his machines.

In night's bull's-eye, I scuttled between windows, creating
                         friendships with chimneys,
   shuttered markets, the foliage of rooftop gardens.

After she died, my mother did not return as I had hoped, so I
                                      continued singing,
   letting my voice bear its sadness over the rooftops, recalling

The conclusion to *The Trial*, when the two gentlemen escort Joseph
                                K. to the killing field
   and let him choose his own knife – as if, by doing him this small
                                        service, they could

Apologize. I ran to the bedroom window: yes, there was the world
   apologizing to me! Smokestacks, steeples, the sky: everything
                                was apologizing to me!

# Fountain of the Planet of the Apes

One by one, they pulled themselves from the water,
slashed their webbed fingers free on coral,
and tore from their necks the few remaining scales.
The scars of gills dissolved from their bare sides.

Their minds dried and took shape. They heaped the island
with signs of their presence, totems of black onyx
from dead volcanic vents. They prayed for children
and children appeared miraculously inside them.

Everything was sacred: beetles, twilight, the law.
Each year, they lit the incense fourteen times.
They loved each other in ways now obvious, quaint,
though others hated them for it and died bitterly

among shifting silk curtains and the odors of smallpox.
Then nothing was sacred, and they filled the cattle-cars
with bewildered people, mile upon mile, receding.
A girl once told me these stories as we lay on her bed.

She said, "Our knowledge removes us from our past,"
and I didn't say, "It also removes us from each other."
I was unsure, in the end, whether it was true
and in the glare of her lamp was afraid to make a mistake.

## Is It the Quiet Mind that Calls

Is it the quiet mind that calls
its sister to the task of conversation?

Is it the venerable feared disease
that draws us in with the harmonies of a siren?

Is it the wheel that flattens the sky,
leaving no mark on the adamant clouds?

Is it the frozen tree that glides
within its enormous cube of water?

Is it the quiet mind that cries
across such distances to reach its brother?

Is it the house whose thin green door
opened a thousand times to let you out?

And others: did they often roll
their words to you down a well-trodden hall –

Words that pinched or stung or consoled,
or swallowed you, majestically, like a father?

And blow by blow, did that five-point star, your hand,
collide with what it could not understand –

The best creatures among us, those who halt
before bright days where nothing must revolt?

# Dreaming in German

These blocks of stone strewn in the abandoned quarry
    testify to the arms' work, not the heart's.
There will be plenty of time for *that* work, after all,
    when the dust of industry settles and our days lie empty.
And decades later, when the rains have finally spilled over the
                                      quarry-mouth,
    if a young teacher from the nearby art college
goes swimming in the gray-green water
    ninety feet above all that half-gnawed rock, who's to say
she hasn't made the worksite into something more profitable?

    Tonight, she dreams she has written the perfect poem.
Its words appear in her head the next morning, in German:
    "Wir kannten nicht sein unerhörtes Haupt." That's the first line,
referring to an ancient piece of statuary
    that, in her dream, is headless. "Darin die Augenäpfel," second
                                                    line,
"in which the eyeballs" of this forgotten head,
    probably destroyed by now
or buried under centuries of rubble, would have gazed out, outlined
    with red ochre, perhaps filled in with blue
or a darker, more costly purple ... The rest of the dream is lost. It's
                                                mid-morning;
    she turns at the sound of the door; the cat peeks in.

Yet these days, with all their distractions, still proffer the odd moment
    that somehow strikes her, as if from memory,
as impossibly consequential, and which remains blinking from the
                                                    branches
    despite all her neglect and the awful weather,
as if *that* were the heart's work – that clever muscle – to memorize
    what otherwise might slip away
in the corridor between sleeping and waking, when the mind is rusty
    as an unused tool. And what could be more precise
than this capacity to pluck instantly from deep waters the silver thread

   of a smell smelled once only, a single minnow
chosen from thousands of others, that curls in the palm
   exactly as before, when it was wet
and still underwater, and she was not simply imagining it?

# Appalachian Diurnal

*When things draw near, or happen, we perceive*
*nothing of them. Except what others bring us*
*we have no news of those who are alive.*

– Dante, *Inferno* X.

    Shade-dampened leaves
snow down on the forest floor. Beyond the wood's wet brake, the
                              strangler fig coiling
    like a tentacle,
a town lies level on a plain of palmetto and furze.
    Its people walk
to the cadence of hymnals. Its streets are delicate as the glass valves
                              of its factories.
    At night, its parks
thicken with dandelion and sprays of false morel.

    These people are civil:
coins fall from their hands in generous showers. They celebrate
                              winter; they write
    biographies of dead relatives;
they harvest ice from the half-frozen ponds, their hooks catching
                              the sunlight
    like the eyes of Argus
opening onto the dawn. When storms sweep in with their million-
                              fingered waves,
    the stubborn town
battens itself and clings like a barnacle. Even the tenements stand
                              fast.
    The soldiers' weapons are clean
and locked in the armory; their trophy heads are neatly piked in the
                              campo.

I face the gashed forest
across its sea of furze. A yellow rail breaks between us, its wings
:::::::::::::::::::::::::::::::::::::::::::::::::::::::::::::::::::::::flashing
   like chasubles.
Smoke has filtered the sun to an orange wafer. If the sky is anything,
   it is a kind of forgetting,
a way of erasing the twisted roots. They populate the soil like worms,
   the hand like handfuls of hair.

# Klintholm Havn

*Denmark*

I have watched the teenagers
late at night, crowding
on the rotted wharves
and in the oystershell
alcoves of the jetties,
smoking vanilla cigarettes,
exhausting their lighters.
When I pass by,
they blink at me
like mute swans.

Tonight, a man is silencing
the lamps along the harbor
one by one, with
a long steel pole.
He walks along the lip
of the sea-wall
like an anachronism.
Behind him, the waves
bare their backs
and melt into foam.

There is no question
of time in this place.
There are only black coffee and oranges,
fried herring
which neither you nor I
can bring ourselves to eat,
and the diminishing
of hopes that, once,
I nursed for us
in this life or another.

IV

# Elegy For J.S. Mill

I. Weighing the Body Politic

a.

Early afternoon.
Reading John Stuart Mill instead of Rousseau.
Rousseau was so afraid of losing his friends
that he did. Mill kept his, and in his books
did not flog himself senseless every page.

I get upset when the coffee cools,
burrow deeper in my plush fauteuil.

I'm like Rousseau, so I read Mill.

b.

My father, a beat policeman, studied law
late into the night as his family slept.

He would wake with the law's heat
shining from his face. I reflected it
in the white fruit of my own.

When I grew mad and horrible at eighteen
and jilted him like some clumsy beloved,
he never said a word, and continued to break eggs
for our elaborate Sunday breakfasts
as if my mother, and I with my mouth of stone,
were either of us completely there.

*Elegy for John Stuart Mill*

c.

In the meat of Mill's chapter on "individuality,
as one of the elements of well-being," I justify
a lunch of wheat-berries and flat soda,
my thumb in the eye of custom's "despotism ...
the tendency of things ... to render mediocrity
the ascendant power among mankind."

The food is a hard horse-pill.
I nailed up the doors and windows
weeks ago, the starting gun
to a marathon of days
spent hide- and house-bound.
Given the choice between sleep and keeping awake,
I choose sleep every night.

Sleep comes easily, like a raveling thread.

d.

Two figures emerge from the fog of my block:
Mill père, and beside him, John Stuart the son
watching his feet with the eyes of a rabbit,
declining Latin nouns in a choirboy-squeak.
They approach like the premises of a syllogism –
Mill *qua* Mill, Father *qua* Father –
arm in arm beneath an iron conclusion
that finds sound logic more persuasive than rhythm.

Their garden snakes sketch amphibrachs
over the path that runs from Pentonville.

*Elegy for John Stuart Mill*

Poor beleaguered Mill. At twenty-one,
sudden neurasthenia (or whatever).
At twenty-four, and for the next half-century,
absolutely blitzed by Harriet Hardy Taylor,
even after her lungs filled up with blood
and her pen splashed down in the midst of his drafts ...

II. J.S. Mill, Fetus

a.

Winter. The light breaking from Essex,
light of my boyhood refracted *ad infinitum,*
enjoins me to compose political letters
until this hand cramps
like a macaque's paw.

b.

Oxbridge could give me nothing
my father had not already.

Thus I settled down to work
among the lowing Brahmans,
the dust and the green tea-fields.

Those were my years of puberty.
Public policy. Sheer wonder
at the power of modern empiricism –
its fingers, gloved in white Calcutta linen,
tracing the humblest of my humble inductions.

*Elegy for John Stuart Mill*

c.

On cloudy days, I cough up teaspoons of blood
and think of Harriet, "whose approbation
was my chief reward." Who – after ten years –
left her orchid-smell to linger in the boudoir,
whose martyr's pallor she could disguise at will
to preserve the air of an MP's wife's card-room.

One does not lead a life of abstention
if one is working hard.
We always did.

And when Disraeli visited, a decade after her death,
I offered him a turtle as if we were Samuel Johnson
and Sir Joseph Banks, and spilled my glass of claret
twice as my body shook from sudden weeping.


d.

Blotting the page, I smear my own name.
In spite of Pope and Sand, our land's first love
is the romance writer wedged in his escritoire,
teeth dripping ink, pen poised, his eyes aglow
with England and the never-setting sun.

I claim the right to ask what we have done
in a voice as clear as a gravestone bell.

*Nothing, by jingo, nothing wrong at all!*

*Elegy for John Stuart Mill*

Well. The truth will out.
The cab-horses will always champ their bits
and steam in the cobblestoned gloom of Fleet Street;
politics will flutter alongside the price of tobacco.

Open the French shutters, lie back in bed.
It is a lung's palette the sunset displays.

e.

In my dream, a red womb curls in a wren's nest.
Another womb rests on a window ledge, like a pie;
others lie strewn along the street.
Nothing comes from them, no motion or sound

suggesting life, but they glow bright,
bright as gaslight. They are a revelation
in concert with itself ...

I turn down the lamp and trim my father's wicks,
watch these wombs until the beeswax pools
like milk on my black-walnut taboret.

And wake to find the candles still burning.
I know nothing. The light I see is not myself
but a similitude, a cobbler's face in the glass,
calling me down from the mountain of my learning.

## Descent

The lights of the tarmac below us.
Ears collapsing, exuberance of pistons,
cherry orchard swarming with baby's breath.
Gray wallpapers in shade, ill-grafted flowers,
the flies that graze from wall to wall,
fists of roots asprawl below rolled turf,
sea sponges moving on an ocean shelf.
Medieval religious paintings, religious frescoes.
Hand-ground pigments. The lame man on his cot
lowered through a hole in the roof.
Guest and host grasping both ends of a doorknob.
A desert outstripping its continent's borders;
bedouins traveling through it with spices and cloths.
Seizures of gnats. Red sweat running
into the Byzantine eyes of Christ
chest-deep in Gethsemane grass: improbable.
Improbable spring, improbable summer.
Pears set out too long on the kitchen table,
chocolates set out too long. A basket
of mustards, cheeses, jams in tiny jars.
Circular rolls of hay – clover, alfalfa –
dotting the square of a sodden field.
Stern professors with ungrateful children.
Wreckage of families batted back and forth.
Sky; violet clouds and cold air. The small,
blue lights of the tarmac beside us.
Strangers' faces in the airport windows.

# Coelacanth

Is it such a crime to stop writing?
We all could burn our manuscripts
and not once dwell on their absence.
The world would be free of poets.
Then I would be at liberty
to sit all day at the kitchen table
carving toys for my children.

How quickly the afternoon fades
when one is well-fed, and has no
elaborate metaphors at his disposal!
Eight o'clock: I turn to the news.
Two Indonesian fishermen
have captured a coelacanth
in the mouth of the Celebes Sea.

# A Note About Matthew Ladd

Matthew Ladd was born in Los Angeles and raised in the Texas Panhandle. After completing his undergraduate work in West Texas, he read for the MPhil in Divinity at the University of Cambridge, submitting a master's thesis on Kierkegaard and German Idealism. In 2006 he received an MFA in Poetry from the University of Florida. His poems have appeared in such journals as the *Paris Review*, *Yale Review*, *Virginia Quarterly* and *Antioch Review*. He has also written criticism for the *American Scholar*, *The Humanist* and the *Threepenny Review*, among other publications, and he writes an annual poetry review for *West Branch*, the literary journal of Bucknell University. He currently lives in New York.

# A Note About the Anthony Hecht Poetry Prize

The Anthony Hecht Poetry Prize was inaugurated in 2005 and is awarded on an annual basis to the best first or second collection of poems submitted.

2005
Judge: J. D. McClatchy
Winner: Morrie Creech, *Field Knowledge*

2006
Judge: Mary Jo Salter
Winner: Erica Dawson, *Big-Eyed Afraid*

2007
Judge: Richard Wilbur
Winner: Rose Kelleher, *Bundle o' Tinder*

2008
Judge: Alan Shapiro
Winner: Carrie Jerrell, *After the Revival*

2009
Judge: Rosanna Warren
Winner: Matthew Ladd, *The Book of Emblems*

For further information, please send an SASE to the press or visit its website:

http://waywiser-press.com/hechtprize.html

# Other books from Waywiser

POETRY

Al Alvarez, *New & Selected Poems*
Robert Conquest, *Penultimata*
Morri Creech, *Field Knowledge*
Peter Dale, *One Another*
Erica Dawson, *Big-Eyed Afraid*
B. H. Fairchild, *The Art of the Lathe*
Jeffrey Harrison, *The Names of Things: New & Selected Poems*
Joseph Harrison, *Identity Theft*
Joseph Harrison, *Someone Else's Name*
Anthony Hecht, *Collected Later Poems*
Anthony Hecht, *The Darkness and the Light*
Carrie Jerrell, *After the Revival*
Rose Kelleher, *Bundle o' Tinder*
Dora Malech, *Shore Ordered Ocean*
Eric McHenry, *Potscrubber Lullabies*
Timothy Murphy, *Very Far North*
Ian Parks, *Shell Island*
Chris Preddle: *Cattle Console Him*
Christopher Ricks, ed. *Joining Music with Reason:
34 Poets, British and American, Oxford 2004-2009*
Daniel Rifenburgh, *Advent*
W.D. Snodgrass: *Not for Specialists: New & Selected Poems*
Mark Strand, *Blizzard of One*
Bradford Gray Telford, *Perfect Hurt*
Cody Walker, *Shuffle and Breakdown*
Deborah Warren, *The Size of Happiness*
Clive Watkins, *Jigsaw*
Richard Wilbur, *Mayflies*
Richard Wilbur, *Collected Poems 1943-2004*
Norman Williams, *One Unblinking Eye*
Greg Williamson, *A Most Marvelous Piece of Luck*

FICTION

Gregory Heath, *The Entire Animal*
Matthew Yorke, *Chancing It*

ILLUSTRATED

Nicholas Garland, *I wish ...*

NON-FICTION

Neil Berry, *Articles of Faith: The Story of British Intellectual Journalism*
Mark Ford, *A Driftwood Altar: Essays and Reviews*
Richard Wollheim, *Germs: A Memoir of Childhood*